Original title:
Holding Onto Stardust

Copyright © 2025 Swan Charm
All rights reserved.

Author: Liina Liblikas
ISBN HARDBACK: 978-9908-1-4498-6
ISBN PAPERBACK: 978-9908-1-4499-3
ISBN EBOOK: 978-9908-1-4500-6

Glittering Hues of Forgotten Nights

In shadows deep where whispers dwell,
A tale unfolds, secrets to tell.
Stars wink softly in the sky,
As dreams of yesteryear float by.

Moonlight dances on silent streams,
Echoing laughter, lost in dreams.
Colors fade, yet memories spark,
Illuminating the once bright dark.

Mist rolls in, a velvet shroud,
Nature sings, both fierce and proud.
Every rustle, a voice of old,
In hues of silver, stories told.

Candles flicker, shadows play,
Carrying echoes of yesterday.
Each glance reveals a hidden glow,
In places where forgotten things flow.

So let us walk these paths anew,
In glittering shades of every hue.
With hearts aligned and spirits free,
We'll find the magic meant to be.

A Journey Toward Celestial Horizons

With every step, the cosmos calls,
Beyond the cliffs and ancient walls.
Stars align in patterns bright,
Guiding travelers through the night.

In the silence of the vast expanse,
We seek the dreams that hold a chance.
Galaxies spin in timeless grace,
Inviting us to join their race.

Nebulas paint the dark with light,
Each hue a story born from flight.
Comets streak with fiery tails,
Whispers of forgotten trails.

As we wander the cosmic seas,
We find our hearts in the gentle breeze.
The universe wraps us in its arms,
A tapestry woven with timeless charms.

So let this journey shape our fate,
Towards horizons, we won't wait.
With eyes aglow and souls ablaze,
We'll dance through this endless maze.

Echoes of Distant Galaxies

Whispers of light from afar,
Dancing in the velvet night.
Tales of stars that once were,
Lost in the cosmic flight.

Muted shadows of the past,
Carry secrets through the void.
Each twinkle a memory cast,
In the silence, we're buoyed.

Nebulas swirling, colors blend,
Stories of time yet untold.
In their beauty, hearts transcend,
In the dark, we are bold.

Fragments of hope in the haze,
Guiding us through time and space.
In their glow, we find our place,
The universe, our embrace.

Through the ages, echoes sing,
Of worlds both near and far.
In the night, our spirits cling,
To the light of a distant star.

Chasing the Ethereal Spark

In the quiet, a flame ignites,
Flickering with an ancient glow.
Chasing whispers of delights,
In the shadows, dreams flow.

Moments linger on the edge,
Awakening the heart's desire.
Each step leads us to the hedge,
Of hope that never tires.

Boundless skies call out our name,
As we dance in the twilight's gleam.
With every heartbeat, we reclaim,
The essence of our dream.

Stars align in secret paths,
Drawing us ever near.
In our laughter, the cosmos laughs,
As we shed the weight of fear.

Awakened by the fervent light,
We venture into the unknown.
With every spark that takes flight,
Our souls find a place called home.

Sculpting Dreams from Cosmic Dust

With hands of stardust, we create,
Woven tales of endless sky.
Molding visions, we await,
As the galaxies drift by.

In the silence, echoes rise,
Casting spells of light and sound.
Imagination never lies,
In the universe, we're found.

From the ashes, new forms grow,
Countless worlds waiting to bloom.
In their essence, we bestow,
Life beyond the empty room.

Each fragment holds a whispered truth,
A memory of distant skies.
In the dreams of ageless youth,
The cosmos' heartbeat lies.

Together we embrace the night,
Sculpting futures, bright and vast.
In the stellar glow, ignite,
A legacy that will last.

Beneath a Canopy of Wishes

Underneath the starry veil,
Wishes dance on moonlit streams.
Every sigh becomes a sail,
Carrying our utmost dreams.

Fleeting moments, soft and clear,
Gathered like the autumn leaves.
In our hearts, the truth is near,
In their rustle, hope believes.

The sky holds each whispered prayer,
Entwined with the night's embrace.
In the stillness, we dare share,
The secrets of hidden grace.

Through the branches, starlight weaves,
A tapestry of endless light.
In the shadow, hope retrieves,
The spark that ignites the night.

So beneath this cosmic dome,
We shall plant our dreams anew.
In the vastness, we find home,
And the universe shines through.

In Pursuit of Celestial Secrets

Stars whisper softly in the night,
Secrets entwined in gentle light.
They dance above in silent grace,
Inviting dreams to find their place.

Planets spin in cosmic ballet,
Each with a story, a path to lay.
Wonders linger in the vast expanse,
Guiding the heart in a timeless dance.

Comets streak with a fiery tail,
Chasing shadows of the moonlit gale.
A symphony of worlds combined,
In the deep abyss of the mind.

Nebulas swirl, colors collide,
Hiding mysteries where shadows abide.
Galaxies bloom like flowers bright,
In the canvas of the infinite night.

So we gaze at the heavens above,
In search of beauty, truth, and love.
Each twinkle holds a whispered fact,
In pursuit of secrets that we attract.

Emblems of the Night Sky

Constellations weave stories old,
Tales of heroes, warriors bold.
A tapestry of dreams drawn wide,
Under stars where memories abide.

The moon, a guardian in the dark,
Casting spells with its silver arc.
Each night it glows, a beacon bright,
Leading wanderers through the night.

Shooting stars, beacons of hope,
Encourage wishes, help us cope.
They leave their trails of burning light,
A fleeting glimpse in the shrouded night.

Planets shine with a steadfast glow,
Their paths entwined in cosmic flow.
Emblems of journeys long and grand,
In the orbit of a silent hand.

We find solace in the vast unknown,
Under the canopy, we are not alone.
In the infinity of the dusky sky,
We seek our purpose, our reason why.

Glimmers of Forgotten Galaxies

In the depths of space, echoes reside,
Tales of worlds that have long since died.
Dust and stars in a serene embrace,
Whispers of life in a timeless space.

Faint outlines of what used to be,
Glimmers tracing history's decree.
Each twinkle tells of love and loss,
Galaxies born, only to toss.

Through telescopes we peer and dream,
At forgotten realms where shadows gleam.
What secrets still lie in their cores?
Unlocking mysteries, opening doors.

Cosmic wonders never cease to amaze,
In the vast blue, we walk through a haze.
Glimmers of beauty, remnants once bright,
Resting in silence, out of our sight.

We chase the echoes, the light from afar,
Each star a story, a hidden memoir.
In the fabric of cosmos, we find our way,
In search of glimmers that silently sway.

A Touch of Cosmic Wonder

Galactic dreams fill the starlit sky,
A painter's canvas where comets fly.
Each stroke a mystery, vast and profound,
A touch of wonder in silence is found.

Celestial orbs in their orbit dance,
Holding secrets in a cosmic trance.
Celestial whispers, soft and clear,
Invite the hearts that dare to steer.

Auroras dance on the edge of night,
A rainbow's glow, a fleeting light.
Drawn in wonder, we pause and stare,
At the universe, wild and rare.

The cosmos pulses with rhythmic flow,
In its embrace, we come to know.
A touch of magic, an endless quest,
In the heart of night, we find our rest.

So let your dreams take to the skies,
Where the cosmos breathes and softly sighs.
With each glance up, may you discover,
A touch of wonder to lift and hover.

Fragments of Interstellar Light

Stars whisper softly in the void,
Silhouettes of dreams, undestroyed.
Galaxies spin in a cosmic dance,
Fragmented moments, a fleeting glance.

Shimmering paths of starlit grace,
Time unfurls in a boundless space.
Each twinkle holds a tale untold,
A universe of wonders bold.

Radiant echoes from realms afar,
Each pulse a sign, a guiding star.
Scattered bits of light entwined,
In the vastness, love defined.

Through the silence, journeys unfold,
In every gleam, a story told.
Fragments dance in the endless night,
Painting dreams with interstellar light.

Dance of the Glittering Veil

Underneath the moon's soft glow,
Winds of mystery gently blow.
Veils of shimmer, ethereal grace,
Invite the starlight to embrace.

Cosmic breezes, ancient songs,
In this dance, where all belong.
Threads of silver, whispers of gold,
Together, secrets to unfold.

Laughter echoes through the dark,
The universe ignites a spark.
As we twirl in celestial play,
In a waltz beneath the Milky Way.

The glittering veil sways and spins,
In cosmic rhythm, love begins.
Every heartbeat a glowing tale,
Lost in the dance of the glittering veil.

Memory's Cosmic Tapestry

Woven threads of starry dreams,
Capture moments, or so it seems.
Memory dances in cosmic light,
Each stitch a whisper, pure delight.

Nebulas cradle the tales of old,
Stories in hues of blue and gold.
Emotions flow like rivers wide,
In this vastness, we take our ride.

Fragments of time, gently embraced,
In the tapestry, dreams interlaced.
Constellations link lost memories,
A cosmic quilt that never flees.

Through the fabric of space and time,
Our hearts beat in perfect rhyme.
In each thread, forever bound,
A universe of love is found.

Fables Woven in Nebulae

In the cradle of nebula's glow,
Fables weave and stories flow.
Galactic tales of heroes bold,
Ancient wisdom, truths retold.

Mysteries float on stardust streams,
Crafting realities from our dreams.
With every hue, a lesson learned,
In the cosmos, passions burned.

Celestial scribes with golden quills,
Ink of starlight, our hearts it fills.
Fables dance in swirling hues,
Guiding seekers with cosmic clues.

From the heart of the astral seas,
Stories rise like fragrant breeze.
In nebula's embrace, we find our place,
Woven fables, bound by grace.

Starlit Pathways of the Heart

Underneath the velvet night,
Whispers dance among the stars,
Guiding souls on endless flight,
Map of dreams, no visible scars.

Footsteps soft on cosmic grass,
Every light a tale to weave,
Paths of love that time won't pass,
In this place, we dare believe.

Moonlit shadows kiss the ground,
Hearts ignite with fleeting glow,
In the silence, love is found,
In the dark, we come to know.

Words unspoken fill the air,
Each heartbeat a celestial spark,
Promises linger everywhere,
Lighting up the endless dark.

Through the maze of stars we roam,
With the night as our embrace,
In this vast and wondrous dome,
We discover our true place.

Treasures Buried in Cosmic Dust

In the depths of endless skies,
Glimmers hide in shadowed haze,
Silent stories, ancient lies,
Waiting for the light to blaze.

Fragments of the past remain,
Crystals gleam in time's own hand,
Echoes of both joy and pain,
Woven deep in stardust sand.

Luminous like dreams once lost,
Each particle a chance to find,
Riddles wrapped in cosmic frost,
Unlocking the paths left behind.

We dig deep with hearts of fire,
Searching for that golden gleam,
To arise and to inspire,
From the whispers of our dreams.

Amidst the chaos, hope prevails,
In the cosmos, treasures gleam,
Journeying beyond the veils,
Awakening all we seem.

The Gentle Touch of Astral Realms

In the cradle of the night,
Soft embraces wrap the soul,
Fingers trace the edge of light,
Bringing peace that makes us whole.

Stars extend a lullaby,
Cradling dreams in cosmic hands,
Where the softest wishes lie,
And the universe understands.

Gentle whispers call us near,
In the quiet, truths unfold,
Casting away every fear,
In the warmth of realms untold.

From the depths of time and space,
Every heartbeat, every breath,
Love is found in every trace,
In the dance of life and death.

Floating in this astral sea,
We become the stars above,
In this moment, we are free,
Touched by the hand of pure love.

Echoes Carried by Stellar Winds

On the breeze of cosmic flight,
Echoes linger, soft and bright,
Tales of hearts that once beat strong,
Whispering in the night's sweet song.

Through the fabric of the void,
Sound of laughter, joy, and fears,
Memories that once enjoyed,
Now woven through the years.

Carried by the winds of fate,
Every note a star's desire,
In this endless dance, we wait,
For the spark to reignite the fire.

Voices echo, soft and clear,
Brushing past the shades of doubt,
In the stillness, love draws near,
In the silence, hear the shout.

So we listen to the skies,
Let the currents guide our way,
In the whispers, truth replies,
In the night, we find our play.

Whispers of Celestial Dreams

In the hush of twilight's breath,
Stars awaken from their rest.
They whisper secrets of the night,
With shimmering tales, ever bright.

Stardust dances in the air,
Cradled softly, light and rare.
Moonbeams weave their silver thread,
A tapestry above our heads.

Galaxies spin in graceful waltz,
Echoes of the universe's pulse.
Each heartbeat shares a cosmic song,
Reminding us we all belong.

Nebulae bloom in colors bold,
Stories of the ages told.
In the quiet, dreams take flight,
As wonders spark the endless night.

So we gather under skies,
With twinkling hopes that never die.
Whispers of celestial schemes,
Guide us through our secret dreams.

Cradling the Essence of Night

In shadows deep, where silence breathes,
The essence of the night weaves.
Wrapped in darkness, calm and sweet,
A world awaits, where heartbeats meet.

Moonlit pools reflect our thoughts,
In this stillness, comfort sought.
Stars like lanterns, guiding ways,
Shimmer softly, lost in praise.

Crickets serenade the dark,
Nature finds a hidden spark.
While dreams like fireflies take flight,
Painting patterns in the night.

Embracing whispers softly shared,
The essence of our souls laid bare.
In solitude, we find our ground,
Cradled where our thoughts abound.

Each sigh reveals the night's deep lore,
Awakening what came before.
In this moment, fleeting, bright,
We treasure the essence of night.

A Tapestry of Cosmic Light

Woven threads of galaxies,
A cosmic dance, a symphony.
Illuminated dreams unfold,
In a silent story, brightly told.

Colors blending, hues of grace,
A timeless voyage, endless space.
Stars align in patterns grand,
A tapestry we may understand.

From quasar bursts to quiet moons,
The universe hums ancient tunes.
Constellations, maps of old,
Charting paths with light like gold.

In every twinkle, hope ignites,
A tapestry of cosmic lights.
Thread by thread, we weave our fate,
In this fabric, we resonate.

Connected by the galaxies near,
Each shining star, a voice sincere.
A cosmic quilt, we share tonight,
Wrapped in warmth, in cosmic light.

Embracing the Glitter of Infinity

In the vastness where dreams collide,
We embrace the glitter, eyes open wide.
Each spark a promise, a story spun,
In the heart of night, we're never done.

Galaxies swirl in a graceful dance,
Inviting us to join the trance.
With every glimmer, a chance to see,
The infinite paths that set us free.

The cosmos whispers, "You are enough,"
In the glitter, a reflection so tough.
We find our place among the stars,
Embracing the beauty within our scars.

Vibrant echoes pull us near,
In every twinkle, dreams appear.
Embracing the night's endless song,
In this space, we all belong.

As time flows like a gentle stream,
We dance together, lost in dream.
The glitter of infinity beckons loud,
In its embrace, we stand so proud.

Fragments of Light Beneath the Horizon

Golden rays slip through the trees,
Painting shadows on the ground.
Whispers of the dawn's soft breeze,
Hope in every light profound.

Colors dance in morning's glow,
Fleeting moments, dreams take flight.
In the stillness, nature's show,
Fragments of light, pure and bright.

Each beam tells a tale untold,
Of journeys past and paths unknown.
In the warmth, we seek the bold,
New beginnings gently sown.

The horizon stretches far and wide,
A canvas where we start anew.
With every step, we turn the tide,
Fragments of dreams in every hue.

So let us walk this tender way,
Beneath the sky, we find our song.
In the light of each new day,
We learn where we truly belong.

Celestial Reflections on Earth's Canvas

Stars adorned the velvet night,
Scattered gems in endless space.
Mirrored pools of silver light,
Nature's masterpiece, embrace.

The moon whispers soft secrets low,
Guiding spirits on their way.
With each pulse, the waters flow,
Earth and sky in grand ballet.

Galaxies spin, forever bright,
In this cosmic dream we find.
Each heartbeat syncs, a shared delight,
Celestial whispers, intertwined.

Reflections on the water's face,
Echoes of a time long past.
In this tranquil, sacred space,
Eternal moments echo fast.

So let your heart be open wide,
To the wonders that unfold.
In every star where dreams abide,
The universe reveals its gold.

Tracing the Footprints of Dreams

In the sands of time, we tread,
Footprints left by hopes and fears.
Each step forward, words unsaid,
Echo softly in our years.

With every dawn, a fresh theme,
Paths unknown await our sight.
Through the haze, we chase a dream,
Guided by the morning light.

Clouds may gather, storms may rise,
But still, we walk, we persevere.
In our hearts, the flame defies,
Fueling visions, crystal clear.

As night descends, we look back,
Tracing patterns in the night.
Every joy and every crack,
Crafted journeys in our sight.

So let us dance on this fine line,
With whispers of the dreams we weave.
For every step, the stars align,
In their embrace, we learn to believe.

Quiet Moments with the Night Sky

Beneath a canopy of dreams,
Silence hangs like tender lace.
Stars alight with gentle beams,
Embrace the stillness, find your grace.

Whispers of the evening breeze,
Cool caress upon the skin.
In this moment, time's at ease,
Quiet thoughts begin to spin.

Constellations guide our gaze,
Stories old in distant light.
In their glow, we weave our praise,
Connecting hearts through the night.

The moon lingers, soft and wise,
Casting shadows, tender glow.
In her presence, secrets rise,
Quiet moments freely flow.

So, let us cherish these deep sighs,
In the night, we find our way.
Underneath the infinite skies,
Together, we shall ever stay.

Dancing with Celestial Fireflies

In the night where fireflies play,
They twinkle bright, lead the way.
A gentle breeze stirs the leaves,
As starlit whispers weave through eaves.

Moonlight flickers on quiet streams,
Casting shadows like soft dreams.
We twirl beneath the glowing charms,
Wrapped in nature's soothing arms.

Each flicker tells a tale untold,
Of ancient magic, brave and bold.
We dance beneath the cosmic glow,
With every heartbeat, soft and slow.

A symphony of light and grace,
In this enchanted, timeless space.
On this night we find our place,
In fireflies' waltz, we interlace.

As dawn approaches, stars retreat,
The world awakes, our hearts still beat.
We'll carry this glow, this gentle fire,
Forever bound to celestial choir.

Beneath the Veil of Distant Skies

Beneath the veil of twilight's sigh,
The stars awaken in the sky.
Each glimmer hugs the passing night,
Leading dreams that take their flight.

A canvas stretched with paints of gold,
Whispers of secrets, tales of old.
We stand in wonder, hearts aligned,
In the allure that fate designed.

Clouds dance softly like drifting thoughts,
Carrying wishes that time forgot.
In this realm where silence soars,
We find ourselves behind closed doors.

To touch the edge of midnight's grace,
Finding solace in this space.
We'll weave our hopes with threads of light,
Beneath the dark, beyond the bright.

As dawn awakens, the magic fades,
But in our hearts, the light cascades.
We'll cherish moments forged in sighs,
Held forever beneath distant skies.

The Embrace of Universe's Shimmer

In the depth of cosmic night,
Galaxies dance, a wondrous sight.
Sparkling dust in silent embrace,
Crafting dreams in boundless space.

Here, the whispers of stars align,
Drawing paths of fate divine.
With every pulse, the heavens sigh,
In this cradle, we learn to fly.

Nebulas bloom with colors bright,
Painting tales of serenity's light.
In the hush of infinity's arms,
We discover life, its endless charms.

Time flows softly, like a stream,
Carrying us through the cosmic dream.
Every moment, a stitch in time,
In this embrace, we find our rhyme.

As the dawn kisses night goodbye,
We hold the universe, you and I.
In shimmer's glow, our spirits soar,
Bound forever, we seek for more.

Sifting Through a Sea of Light

In the dawn where shadows fade,
We sift through light, a golden cascade.
Each ray a promise, warm and bright,
Guiding us through the morning light.

Amidst the glow of waking dreams,
We discover truth in sunlit beams.
With every step, the world awakes,
Filling hearts with joy it makes.

The breeze whispers secrets untold,
In its embrace, we find the bold.
Each moment a drop in the sea,
Of light that sets our spirits free.

A dance of echoes, soft and clear,
The heart sings what the soul holds dear.
In this journey, we find our sight,
As we sift through the sea of light.

As day gives way to evening's glow,
We carry the warmth, allow it to flow.
With hands held tight, we journey on,
Sifting dreams until the dawn.

Luminance in the Depths of Space

In the silence of vast night,
Stars whisper secrets bright.
Nebulas glow with ancient tales,
Their light a dance, a cosmic sail.

Planets spin in endless grace,
Each a dream, a timeless place.
Galaxies swirl in a grand display,
Their beauty put on full array.

Comets blaze through darkened skies,
With tails that shimmer and rise.
In the depths, the voids collide,
Yet within them, wonders hide.

Light years pass in fleeting thought,
Many truths in darkness caught.
Eclipses mask the glowing face,
Yet hope prevails in every space.

Infinite realms of soft embrace,
Infinity's comforting lace.
We reach out to touch the divine,
In the depths, the stars align.

Dreams that Sparkle Like Stars

In twilight's hush, dreams take flight,
Glimmers in the velvety night.
A tapestry of hope unfolds,
Stories of the brave and bold.

Each thought a star, igniting skies,
Flickering fiercely, never dies.
In every pulse, our wishes gleam,
Across the universe, we dream.

Moments linger like stardust trails,
Whispers of fate in cosmic gales.
Veiled in shimmer, mysteries call,
We find our paths where shadows fall.

Transcending time, love's gentle spark,
Illuminates the endless dark.
Every heartbeat echoes through,
These dreams, our universe anew.

Hope ignites with every dawn,
Across the night, our spirits drawn.
Beneath vast skies, we lift our gaze,
In dreams, we find our endless ways.

The Fluidity of Celestial Wishes

Wishes float on cosmic streams,
Carried by gentle stardust gleams.
In the realm of a midnight sigh,
They swirl and dance, then drift on high.

Like rivers through the galactic expanse,
They weave through fate in a timeless dance.
Ephemeral, yet fiercely bright,
Guiding hearts through the infinite night.

With each breath, a new wish flies,
Echoing soft in the endless skies.
A promise made on astral waves,
A legacy within starlit caves.

Yearning whispers echo through space,
In the heartbeat of this vast place.
Cascading dreams, like falling stars,
Transform the night into memoirs.

Fluid dreams across the dark,
Carry forth an eternal spark.
In the cosmos, alive and free,
Wishes flow, as meant to be.

A Galaxy of Unwritten Stories

Hidden realms of thought and lore,
A galaxy waits, yearning for more.
With every soul, a tale unwinds,
Intertwining hearts and minds.

Chapter by chapter, stars align,
Crafting voyages through space and time.
In silence, whispers grasp the night,
Unseen dramas, set to ignite.

Nebulae cradle dreams untold,
Each shimmer a secret to behold.
In cosmic dust, we search, we roam,
Finding paths that lead us home.

The moon conceals its tales with care,
While constellations spin truths rare.
Footprints marked in the sands of fate,
Breathe life into stories innate.

We are the scribes of starlit pages,
Each heartbeat, a verse transcends ages.
In this galaxy of endless schemes,
We pen our lives through vibrant dreams.

Whispers of Celestial Dreams

In silence, stars begin to hum,
Soft echoes of the night's sweet song.
A tapestry of dreams unfolds,
Where wishes linger, bright and strong.

The moonlight dances on the waves,
A shimmer on the tranquil sea.
Lost thoughts drift like autumn leaves,
In the embrace of reverie.

Galaxies swirl in a gentle breeze,
Carrying secrets from afar.
Each spark ignites a tale of hope,
Under the watch of the morning star.

In realms where starlit visions play,
Life's canvas stretches wide and vast.
We weave our dreams with tender threads,
Creating futures from the past.

So close your eyes and take the flight,
To worlds where every heart can gleam.
In whispers soft, the night reveals,
The beauty found in celestial dreams.

Glimmers in the Night Sky

Above, the heavens shine so bright,
With whispers of the past entwined.
Each twinkle holds a secret wish,
A glimmer of what's yet to find.

The constellations tell their tales,
Of lovers lost, of battles won.
In silver threads, our hopes converge,
A glowing dance, the night's undone.

Like diamonds scattered on a veil,
Each star ignites the dreams we crave.
They beckon us to reach and grasp,
The universe, our silent wave.

As shadows play upon the ground,
The moon watches, a guardian wise.
With every breath, a spark ascends,
In the embrace of midnight skies.

So let your heart be light and free,
In this vast expanse, you'll fly high.
For in the galaxy's embrace,
Are endless glimmers in the night sky.

Embers of Cosmic Wishes

In the void, the embers glow,
Faint whispers of what once was bright.
Each spark a wish, a silent plea,
Igniting dreams throughout the night.

Across the cosmos, wishes soar,
Like fireworks against the dark.
In every heartbeat, hopes collide,
Creating constellations, a spark.

These embers dance in cosmic wind,
Fleeting moments, brief and rare.
They carry stories from the stars,
Of love and loss, of joy, despair.

Each flicker holds a tale untold,
Of souls who sailed through time and space.
A cosmic quilt of light and dreams,
Embracing all in its soft grace.

So gather round and feel the warmth,
Of every wish that brightly burns.
In each small ember lies a flame,
Where cosmic wishes twist and turn.

Embrace of the Astral Glow

In twilight's hush, a glow descends,
A gentle kiss upon the skin.
The astral dreams begin to weave,
A tapestry where hearts can spin.

With every pulse, the universe,
Reveals its secrets, old and grand.
In cosmic dance, we find our place,
Together, held by starlight's hand.

Each moment spent beneath the stars,
A whisper shared, a promise made.
In silence, souls become entwined,
In twilight's glow, no fears invade.

As dawn approaches, colors bloom,
The astral embrace lingers near.
In every breath, we feel the pulse,
Of dreams that flourish, crystal clear.

So take a step into the light,
Let go of all that weighs you down.
In this embrace, we learn to fly,
Where hearts and stars forever crown.

A Canvas Streaked with Cosmic Light

Stars whisper secrets bright,
As galaxies drift through the night.
A canvas painted in hues divine,
Where stardust and silence intertwine.

Nebulas swirl in a cosmic dance,
Each twinkle a fleeting chance.
Across the dark, the colors blend,
Life's mysteries begin and end.

Planets spin, a celestial play,
In this vast theater, night and day.
Comets trace paths of glowing fire,
Awakening dreams, igniting desire.

In the expanse where shadows fall,
The universe beckons, calls us all.
It tells of journeys far and wide,
On this stellar ocean, we glide.

A canvas streaked with endless gleam,
Embracing wonder, we dare to dream.
In the light of the cosmic veil,
We find our story, our destined trail.

Beneath the Milky Veil

Under the arch of a velvet sky,
Whispers of stars, a soft lullaby.
Beneath the Milky Veil, I stand,
Awed by the wonders, vast and grand.

The galaxy swirls in a timeless trance,
In the cosmic sea, we find our chance.
Each shining point a tale untold,
Of love and loss, of brave and bold.

Softly the moonbeams kiss the ground,
In the stillness, beauty is found.
Beneath the canvas of night's embrace,
Is where we gather, a sacred space.

Celestial dreams glimmer and sway,
Guiding the heart along the way.
The stars above in their eternal flight,
Mark the passage of time in the night.

Beneath the Milky Veil, we hold,
Secrets of the universe, bright and bold.
With every breath, we feel its call,
Together we rise, together we fall.

The Dance of Twinkling Memories

In the twilight glow, memories play,
Dancing like fireflies at the end of day.
Each twinkle a sparkle, alive and true,
Whispers of laughter, of me and you.

With every heartbeat, the past unfolds,
Stories of warmth and love retold.
In the dance of shadows, we find our way,
Through the corridors of yesterday.

Moments drift by like leaves on a stream,
Carried away on the wings of a dream.
Captured in time, they sweetly ignite,
The canvas of life, a shimmering light.

As the stars shimmer with tales of old,
We cherish the warmth that memories hold.
In this gentle waltz of joy and pain,
We gather the echoes, like gentle rain.

The dance of twinkling memories flows,
In the heart's embrace, true love knows.
Together we twirl in the night's gentle air,
In every heartbeat, we find a prayer.

Captured Dreams Floating Away

In the quiet dawn, dreams take flight,
Borne by whispers of the night's light.
Captured in hearts, they shimmer and sway,
Like petals unfurling, they float away.

Through valleys of hope, they gently glide,
On currents of wishes, side by side.
In the tapestry woven with threads of night,
Lie fragments of dreams, pure delight.

With each fleeting moment, they drift afar,
Guided by starlight, each shining star.
Captured dreams whisper to the soul,
Filling the void, making us whole.

Though some may vanish on morning's breath,
The echoes remain, a dance with death.
In the realm of longing, they softly play,
Chasing the shadows, they fade away.

Captured dreams, in the light of day,
Guide us gently on our way.
Though they may float like clouds at dusk,
In our hearts, their magic we trust.

When Wishes Fall Like Raindrops

Wishes descend like gentle rain,
Softly falling, easing pain.
Each droplet a hope, a silent plea,
Whispered dreams for you and me.

In puddles they dance, reflections bright,
Mirroring hearts in the fragile light.
Every splash a moment, a fleeting thrill,
A cascade of wishes, time to fill.

As they gather on leaves, so green,
Secret stories in silence glean.
Nature listens, embraces our call,
For in the end, we find them all.

So let the rain bring forth the night,
Each wish a star in fading light.
In the quiet, our hearts align,
When wishes fall, hope entwines.

As dusk merges with dawn's sweet grace,
Wishes dissolve, leave no trace.
Yet in our hearts, they'll always stay,
A glimmer of hope, come what may.

Timeless Comets in Our Souls

Comets streak across the sky,
Marking paths where dreams can fly.
In the silence, we hear their song,
Whispers of where our hearts belong.

Each tail a tale, a wish unseized,
A light that flickers, hearts appeased.
Timeless journeys in cosmic flight,
Our souls ignite with their soft light.

Fleeting moments, they guide our way,
In the vastness, they lead us astray.
But in the chase, we find our role,
Chasing comets that honor the soul.

In twilight's embrace, let us dare,
Dream of comets, send our prayer.
Together we weave through the astral folds,
Holding tight to timeless souls.

As light years pass, still we roam,
Chasing whispers that guide us home.
In every spark, in every glow,
Timeless comets we shall know.

Reveries Under Astral Canopies

Beneath the stars, our dreams take flight,
Wrapped in reveries, soft and light.
The heavens whisper secrets bold,
In the dark, our hopes unfold.

Constellations form in endless night,
Stories woven from shards of light.
In stillness, we linger, heartbeats calm,
Cradled in night's gentle balm.

Every twinkle, a tale to tell,
Of loves transcending, where shadows dwell.
Underneath the astral veil,
We find our paths, we cannot fail.

As galaxies spin, we breathe as one,
Lost in thoughts beneath the sun.
In the vastness, we'll always roam,
Finding solace in the stars we call home.

So let the cosmos be our guide,
In reveries where dreams reside.
With every night, our spirits soar,
Under astral canopies, forevermore.

Veils of Celestial Whimsy

Veils of stardust, soft and bright,
Draped around the moonlit night.
Whimsy dances on the breeze,
Whispers held in cosmic trees.

In realms where fantasies collide,
Celestial wonders are our guide.
Each star a flicker of dreams untold,
In the universe's arms, we'll be bold.

Ethereal laughter fills the air,
Twinkling lights take away our care.
In dreams we wander, hearts aglow,
Veils of whimsy, a gentle flow.

With every pulse of the nightime sky,
Our spirits rise, learn to fly.
Weaving stories through time and space,
In cosmic dreams, we find our place.

So let the universe spin and sway,
In its embrace, we choose to stay.
Veils of whimsy, forever weave,
In celestial realms, we shall believe.

Capture the Faintest Radiance

In twilight's gentle embrace, it glows,
A whisper of warmth that softly flows.
Each fleeting spark, a secret kept,
In shadows deep where silence crept.

The stars above, like scattered dreams,
Illuminate the night with their gleams.
We reach for light, yet fear the fall,
In the quiet moments, we hear the call.

Faint radiance dances on the skin,
A soft reminder of where we've been.
With every breath, a spark ignites,
As echoes linger in the nights.

Through dusky paths, our visions roam,
Finding solace in the unknown.
In whispers shared beneath the skies,
Our hearts' reflections, where truth lies.

Embracing light in shadows' grace,
We capture each illuminating trace.
A journey written in starry lines,
In the faintest glow, our spirit shines.

Ephemeral Threads of Light

In morning mist, a shimmer bright,
Threads of gold weave through the light.
They dance around with fleeting grace,
Moments cherished, a warm embrace.

Each ray a story, a dream untold,
Ephemeral whispers, gentle and bold.
They guide us through the day's first sigh,
In luminous paths, our hopes can fly.

As daylight wanes, the colors blend,
Threads of light that never end.
We chase the sun, a timeless chase,
In fleeting shadows, we find our place.

Soft twilight drapes the world in hues,
Ephemeral echoes of vibrant views.
In every glimmer, a truth will spark,
The essence of life, igniting the dark.

Through nights so still, we reach for dreams,
In fragile threads, our spirit beams.
Dancing softly in the dazzle's flight,
We weave our hopes in threads of light.

Serenade of the Starlit Heart

Underneath the starry quilt,
A serenade of dreams is built.
With every twinkle, hearts take flight,
In the embrace of the velvet night.

Soft melodies the cosmos sings,
Each note a feather, on bright wings.
They echo hopes and secrets shared,
In the starlit dance, we've dared.

Whispers carried on silken breeze,
Serenades play through moonlit trees.
With every pulse, the galaxies hum,
A rhythm where our souls become.

In the vast expanse, where dreams ignite,
We lose ourselves in the purest light.
With every gaze up to the skies,
Our hearts awaken, and love never dies.

Through cosmic chords that pull us near,
The serenade sings, forever clear.
As starlit paths unfold their art,
We find our truth in the starlit heart.

Stardust Footprints on the Moon

In the silence of the lunar glow,
Footprints linger, tales to sow.
Each step a mark on ancient land,
In stardust dreams, we take our stand.

The cosmos whispers in every grain,
A dance through time, a fleeting chain.
With every leap, our spirits soar,
On lunar seas, we long for more.

Curved horizons call our name,
In celestial silence, we play the game.
Beneath the stars, with hearts aglow,
We share the light in midnight's flow.

With every breath, the cosmos sighs,
In moonlit valleys, where wonder lies.
Our stardust footprints tell the tale,
Of journeys vast, where dreams prevail.

Through galaxies wide, we wander free,
Chasing echoes of eternity.
On the moon's face, our hearts entwined,
In stardust paths, our souls aligned.

Echoes of the Ethereal

Whispers dance in twilight's grace,
Fleeting shadows, dreams embrace.
Stars alight in velvet skies,
Echoes of the night arise.

Moonlit paths where spirits roam,
In the silence, find a home.
Threads of fate, the cosmos weave,
In the heart, we dare believe.

Veils of mist, ethereal glow,
Where forgotten secrets flow.
Softly glowing, kindred fires,
Stir the depths of ancient desires.

Through the dark, a melody,
Carried forth by destiny.
In this dance of light and shade,
Echoes linger, never fade.

On the edge of dreams we stand,
Reaching forth with open hand.
In the night, our souls unite,
In the echoes of the light.

Chasing the Celestial Dawn

Glimmers rise on horizon's edge,
Painting skies with vibrant pledge.
Chasing forth the morning's glow,
In the stillness, hearts do grow.

With each ray, a story spun,
Wrapped in warmth, the day begun.
Dreams awaken, courage swells,
In the dawn, the spirit dwells.

Whispers of the night rescind,
Hope and light, the souls rescind.
With the sun, a promise bright,
Guiding paths in morning light.

Clouds of silken, amber hue,
Bathe the world in promise true.
Through the shadows, we will rise,
Chasing forth to azure skies.

Moments fleeting, yet so vast,
Embrace the present, hold it fast.
In each dawn, a chance to find,
Chasing dreams that night left behind.

Threads of an Astral Serenade

In the night, the stars align,
Casting spells, a dance divine.
Melodies in cosmic flight,
Threads of dreams weave through the night.

Softly sung by distant spheres,
Carried forth throughout the years.
In the silence, lullabies,
Cradle hopes beneath the skies.

Shimmering notes of liquid light,
Echoing through the endless night.
Each vibration a gentle tune,
Woven deep, beneath the moon.

Galaxies spin in boundless grace,
In their embrace, we find our place.
Together lost in this charade,
Drawing near with each serenade.

Awakening in twilight's glow,
Hearts entwined in the ebb and flow.
Stars above, a guiding hand,
Threads of fate, we understand.

Capturing the Glow of Evenings Past

Faded whispers in the breeze,
Capture moments, memories tease.
Golden hues, the sunset casts,
Weaving shadows of evenings past.

Where laughter lingered, time stood still,
In the twilight, echoes thrill.
Painting skies in shades of red,
All the words that once were said.

Each tender glance, a fleeting spark,
Illuminating paths through dark.
In the evening's gentle sigh,
Old flames dance and never die.

Carried forth on whispered dreams,
Beneath the stars, the soft moonbeams.
Capturing the glow we chase,
In every memory, every space.

Threads of time, we hold them dear,
In the glow, we draw them near.
Let the night unveil its art,
Capturing the glow in heart.

Secrets Hidden in Light's Embrace

In shadows deep, whispers hide,
A dance of thoughts, the worlds collide.
Silent truths in glimmers play,
Eclipsed by night, yet bright as day.

In every glance, a story spun,
In every heartbeat, secrets run.
Light weaves dreams in golden threads,
While the heart knows what it dreads.

Through the mist, a soft light glows,
Where it leads, nobody knows.
Embrace the warmth, let it unveil,
The hidden paths where shadows pale.

In the depths, a flicker stirs,
A flash of truth, the mind confers.
Yet in that light, a veil still stays,
Holding tightly to our ways.

So let us breathe this mystic air,
Where light and dark together share.
For in their marriage, fate will write,
The secrets wrapped in light's delight.

The Heartbeat of the Universe

In cosmic waves, a rhythm lies,
A pulse that echoes through the skies.
Stars are born, then fade away,
Yet in their light, life finds its way.

Galaxies spin in silent dance,
In every swirl, an unseen chance.
Gravity binds, while light breaks free,
A tapestry of you and me.

Whispers of atoms, soft and low,
In every heartbeat, energy flows.
From endless dark to brilliant hue,
This universe whispers, "I see you."

In the stillness, a spark ignites,
Dreams collide in the starry nights.
Each spark a wish, each wish a tune,
Sung by the night, beneath the moon.

Awake to find the cosmic call,
In every rise, and every fall.
For in each breath, we play our part,
The universe beats within the heart.

Evenings Wrapped in Celestial Touch

Twilight whispers, soft and sweet,
As daylight fades, the stars entreat.
In velvet skies, their jewels gleam,
Woven light in a nightly dream.

Crickets sing their evening tune,
Beneath the watchful silver moon.
Soft shadows dance on quiet streams,
While nature breathes in gentle dreams.

Amongst the trees, a rustle stirs,
The day resigns, the night occurs.
Every breeze brings tales of old,
In whispers soft, and secrets bold.

The horizon blushes, kissing night,
With hues that blend, a pure delight.
Stars awaken, one by one,
Embracing dusk, where day is done.

So let us pause to feel the grace,
Of evenings wrapped in time and space.
For in this moment, quiet and hushed,
The heart and universe are brushed.

Embracing Light's Eternal Gaze

Within the dawn, a promise glows,
A radiant kiss where morning flows.
Embracing light that sweeps the skies,
Awakening truth, where hope lies.

Each day unfolds, a gentle sigh,
As sunbeams dance and shadows fly.
In every ray, a chance to grow,
A journey begun, a path to know.

Through every trial, light remains,
A guiding star through joys and pains.
With every step, we find our way,
In love's embrace, we choose to stay.

Time marches on, yet light stays bright,
In every heart, it ignites the night.
We seek the warmth, the glow, the fire,
To embrace our dreams, to reach higher.

So here we stand, beneath the sky,
In light's embrace, we learn to fly.
For in that gaze, our spirits rise,
To find the truth in love's replies.

Chasing Shadows of Light

In the twilight's golden glow,
Shadows dance, ebb and flow.
Whispers of the day retreat,
As night unveils its secret beat.

Stars awaken, dreams take flight,
Chasing shadows, seeking light.
Every flicker, a chance to see,
The beauty that sets our spirits free.

Through the darkness, we will roam,
Finding paths that lead us home.
In the echo of the night,
We grasp the shadows of pure light.

Fleeting moments, we embrace,
In the silent, sacred space.
Where dreams and shadows intertwine,
We discover what is truly divine.

As dawn arrives, we stand amazed,
In the sunlight's warmth, we're praised.
Chasing shadows, we have learned,
Light within us always yearned.

Eternal Echoes of a Starlit Dream

In the cosmos, dreams arise,
Stars reflect in endless skies.
Eternal whispers in the night,
Guide us through the gentle light.

Softly twinkling, tales unfold,
Of adventures brave and bold.
Each heartbeat an echoing song,
In the starlit realm, we belong.

Time stands still, a fleeting kiss,
In the dreamscape's tender bliss.
Moments woven, forever dear,
Echoes resound for all to hear.

Journey through the astral maze,
Finding peace in cosmic ways.
With each star, a promise gleams,
In the ballet of our dreams.

Let the night be our embrace,
In the dance of time and space.
Eternal echoes call us near,
In starlit dreams, we conquer fear.

A Symphony of Cosmic Whispers

In the stillness, whispers sound,
A symphony where dreams are found.
Galaxies swirl in perfect tune,
Guiding hearts beneath the moon.

Every note, a story plays,
In the vastness, a cosmic blaze.
Melodies of stars align,
Resonating, our souls entwine.

Beats of the universe arise,
Composing truths beyond the skies.
With each breath, we listen close,
To the whispers that we cherish most.

Harmony in shadows cast,
Echoes of the ages past.
In the silence, we are free,
To hear the cosmic symphony.

Together we shall drift away,
In the music that shall stay.
A timeless dance, a celestial song,
In cosmic whispers, we belong.

The Essence of Dreams Written in Light

In pure light, our dreams ignite,
Whispers of hope take flight.
Painting skies with vibrant hues,
In the essence of all we choose.

With every dawn, potential stirs,
In the silence, the heart concurs.
Illuminated paths we chase,
Finding purpose in this space.

Woven threads of night and day,
Guiding our steps, come what may.
In the flicker of every spark,
Dreams come alive, igniting the dark.

Through shadows cast and daylight gleamed,
We seek the truth within our dreams.
In the brilliance, we are found,
The essence of light, profound.

So let us dance in radiant beams,
Living out our wildest dreams.
With every heartbeat, shining bright,
In the essence of dreams, we take flight.

The Glow of Memories Lost and Found

In shadows deep where whispers sigh,
Flickering lights of days gone by.
Echoes dance in twilight's embrace,
Carved in time, the fleeting trace.

Through tangled paths, I wander still,
Chasing thoughts, a fervent thrill.
Soft reminders of love once bright,
In every corner, a soft light.

Laughter lingers like fragrant blooms,
Filling spaces, igniting rooms.
Threads of joy in a tapestry spun,
Weaving moments, forever young.

Tears may fall like autumn leaves,
Yet in sorrow, a heart believes.
From ashes rise the vibrant hues,
Of cherished dreams, and life renews.

In every corner, a story found,
A tapestry where love is bound.
Though time may steal, it can't erase,
The glow of memories, a warm embrace.

Journeying Beyond the Night

On velvet wings, the stars ignite,
Guiding souls through endless night.
Whispers of dreams in the cool, soft air,
Inviting hearts to journey there.

Each step echoes with ancient lore,
Paths of starlight to explore.
The moon weaves silver in the dark,
Sparking hope, a glowing arc.

Lost in wonder, the shadows play,
Painting visions that drift away.
In nebulas of thought and space,
We find ourselves in timeless grace.

Beyond the horizon, where secrets lie,
Every heartbeat, a gentle sigh.
As dawn approaches, the night takes flight,
We journey on, embracing light.

In every dream, a tale unfolds,
Of courage found and daring bold.
Together we tread, hearts entwined,
Journeying beyond, the stars aligned.

Dreamscapes of Celestial Reflections

In realms where stars softly gleam,
Awakening whispers of a dream.
Mirrored skies hold secrets untold,
Celestial wonders, a sight to behold.

Reflections dance on ethereal streams,
Flowing gently, weaving dreams.
Beneath the veil of night's embrace,
We find solace in this sacred space.

Waves of light, a cosmic tide,
Guiding us where hopes abide.
In every flicker, a story spun,
Of lovers lost and battles won.

Galaxies swirl in a timeless waltz,
Embracing shadows without faults.
In the silence, our spirits soar,
Through dreamscapes rich with lore.

So let us drift on this mystic flight,
Hand in hand, through the velvet night.
With every breath, the universe calls,
In celestial depth, the heart enthralls.

Celestial Notions of Tomorrow

In the cradle of dawn, a whisper glows,
Painting hopes where the soft wind blows.
With every sunrise, dreams reawaken,
In celestial realms, there's no mistaking.

Visions rise like the morning light,
Chasing shadows, igniting sight.
In vibrant hues, the day unfolds,
Scripted in stardust, the future holds.

Threads of silver, woven with care,
Carry whispers of what will be there.
Each heartbeat echoes with promise true,
A dance of fate, the old and new.

Let the universe guide our way,
As we embrace the light of day.
Through valleys deep and mountains high,
Celestial notions in every sky.

With open arms, we greet the dawn,
In each heartbeat, a new hope drawn.
Together we'll carve a path divine,
In the tapestry of space and time.

Traces of Astral Melodies

In the twilight where stars collide,
Whispers of time begin to glide,
Amongst the echoes of distant song,
A symphony sweet where dreams belong.

Floating notes in the cosmic sea,
Dance in rhythms so wild and free,
Each beat a story carved in night,
Painting the dark with silver light.

Galaxies weave in gentle embrace,
Tales of wonder, a boundless space,
Frequencies pulse with a timeless grace,
In this harmony, we find our place.

Through nebulae, our spirits soar,
Searching for magic in the lore,
Each twinkle a promise, a wish, a prayer,
Inviting stardust, glimmering air.

Merging paths in celestial dance,
A journey begun with every glance,
Notes of love in the ether sway,
As traces of melodies drift away.

Notes from the Universe's Lullaby

Cradled beneath the vast expanse,
Silent lullabies begin to dance,
Soft as whispers from ancient stars,
Nurturing dreams that heal our scars.

Moments drift in the cosmic sea,
Carried on winds of eternity,
Each note a heartbeat, bold and bright,
Guiding us gently through the night.

Serenades from the night's embrace,
Wrap us in warmth, a softened grace,
Echoes of love in a tender sigh,
Reaching through realms where shadows lie.

Harmonies played by celestial hands,
The universe sings, and the heart understands,
With every star, a tale unfolds,
In the lullaby of the night, it holds.

Rest in the glow of twilight's art,
Let the rhythm soothe your weary heart,
For in the quiet, peace shall arise,
As the universe sings, beneath the skies.

Flickers of Light in the Dark

In the silence of the midnight hour,
Shadows bloom like the night's flower,
Flickers of light begin to play,
Chasing the dark, keeping fear at bay.

Emerging from worlds beyond our sight,
Glimmers dance, inviting the night,
Each spark a promise, whispering truth,
Stirring the echoes of age-old youth.

Stars ignite in a tapestry bright,
Painting hopes with a brush of light,
In their glow, our spirits unite,
Flickers of warmth, banishing night.

Celestial fires in boundless skies,
Witness the beauty with wondrous eyes,
Fleeting moments, but deeply felt,
In the dark, our dreams are dealt.

Catch the essence of the glow so rare,
Enveloped in magic, we find our lair,
For flickers of light are love's true spark,
Guiding our hearts throughout the dark.

Cosmic Remnants of a Dream

In the silence where shadows weave,
Cosmic remnants of dreams believe,
Threads of stardust stretch and flow,
Binding the past to the seeds we sow.

Echoes carried on the solar breeze,
Whispering secrets among the trees,
Each fragment a story of what was born,
In the cradle of stars, our spirits worn.

Galactic whispers speak of the night,
Tales of wonder wrapped in soft light,
Summoning visions from realms unseen,
In the tapestry woven of dreams pristine.

Brushed by the hand of cosmic fate,
Every remnants radiates, resonates,
A dance of memories held so dear,
In the pulse of the universe, ever near.

Rest easy, for dreams shall not fade,
In cosmic realms where memories wade,
Born anew in celestial streams,
We find ourselves in the cosmic dreams.

Light Years Away from Forgetting

In the quiet of night, stars gleam,
Echoes of laughter, lost in a dream.
Whispers of time flow like a stream,
Moments ungrasped, a fragile theme.

Faint shadows dance in the fading light,
Memories flicker, held ever so tight.
Time stretches forth, a marvelous sight,
Carried by winds of eternal flight.

We wander, we search, through vast cosmic bays,
Each heartbeat a map, each breath a phrase.
Caught in the yearning of those brighter days,
We're light years away, lost in their gaze.

Yet in the stillness, they linger near,
Every soft whisper, every sweet tear.
Though the past may shimmer, unclear,
We hold the love, forever sincere.

The universe spins, yet here we remain,
Dancing with shadows of joy and pain.
For time may bend, but love shall sustain,
In starlit echoes, we're whole once again.

The Silken Threads of Infinity

Woven together, time and space,
Silken threads that warm the embrace.
Destinies twist in a cosmic lace,
A tapestry rich, no trace to efface.

Journeys unfold like delicate blooms,
Stars in the night shine, melting the glooms.
Ever entwining, our heartbeats resume,
In the vast silence, the universe looms.

Beneath the vastness, hopes softly glide,
Through nebulous dreams where secrets reside.
With every heartbeat, with every stride,
We touch the infinite, in love we confide.

Fleeting moments, like whispers in air,
Entwined in thoughts, in a dance we share.
In this grand weave, together we dare,
To find our place with delicate care.

The fabric of space holds whispers of fate,
A timeless embrace, we joyfully navigate.
In the endless expanse, we celebrate,
The silken threads that love can create.

Starry-Eyed Wanderings

With eyes turned upward, spirits align,
Galaxies swirl, in patterns divine.
The wondrous sky is a canvas so fine,
Each star a story, in silence they shine.

We wander through cosmos, hand in hand,
Exploring the wonders where dreams expand.
Every comet's trail, a song so grand,
We dance on the edges of galaxies planned.

In the hush of the night, our dreams take flight,
Guided by starlight, a beacon so bright.
Together we roam in the velvet twilight,
In the realms of the infinite, love ignites.

Thoughts drift like clouds, floating through air,
Carried by wishes, so light and rare.
In the heart of the universe, we lay bare,
Our souls intertwined, a journey we share.

Starry-eyed wanderers, we'll never grow old,
In the soft glow of night, our stories unfold.
With each twinkling light, new hopes we hold,
A galaxy's embrace, a tale to be told.

The Memory of Celestial Reflections

In mirrored realms where shadows play,
Celestial whispers guide our way.
Fragments of light, like the break of day,
Reflecting our souls, come what may.

Glimmers of past in the cosmic sea,
Each wave a reminder of what used to be.
In reflections of love, we're nourishing free,
A dance with the stars, just you and me.

The sky paints pictures in colors untold,
Fragments of time, both gentle and bold.
In the quiet of night, the universe unfolds,
Stories of dreams in its grasp to hold.

Through darkened voids, our memories gleam,
A tapestry woven from hopes and dreams.
In celestial corridors, nothing's as it seems,
Embracing the shades of our heart's silent screams.

Like echoes of laughter that softly decay,
The memories linger, they refuse to sway.
In the realms of stardust, come dance, let's play,
In celestial reflections, forever we stay.

An Odyssey Through Cosmic Whispers

In the silence of dark space,
Stars weave tales of hidden grace.
Galaxies spin with whispered dreams,
Echoing soft, celestial themes.

A journey through the astral light,
Where time and age blur out of sight.
Comets blaze with fervent glow,
Painting skies with tales below.

Nebulas swirl in colors bright,
Fingers of dust, a painter's delight.
Each twinkle sings a cosmic song,
In the void where we all belong.

Planets dance in silent waltz,
A ballet of worlds, their faults.
Through the abyss of cosmic night,
We find our way, we seek the light.

An odyssey of thoughts so deep,
In the cosmos, secrets keep.
Travelers of a stardust sea,
In whispers vast, we roam, we free.

Time Wandering through Celestial Veils

Time drifts softly through the stars,
Leaving whispers, ancient scars.
Each moment wrapped in cosmic lace,
An ethereal, timeless space.

Veils of light, like silken dreams,
Shimmer through the world it seems.
We wander lost in a twinkling maze,
Caught in time's elusive gaze.

Galaxies turn in endless flight,
Chasing shadows, embracing light.
Every heartbeat echoes through,
The vastness of the cosmic hue.

Chronicles of ages old,
Stories of the brave and bold.
In the cosmic fabric spun,
Life is woven, all is one.

So we tread the starry night,
Guided by the moon's soft light.
Time may wander, yet we'll find,
The beauty of the cosmic mind.

The Soft Breath of Distant Suns

A breath from stars, both near and far,
Whispers secrets of who we are.
Softly glowing in the night,
Each sun a beacon, pure delight.

From planets sworn to orbit true,
Their warmth extends, a cosmic view.
Wrapped in silk of radiant glow,
Their soft breath helps our spirits grow.

In silence, the universe sighs,
Tales emerge from swirling skies.
Stardust dances on a breeze,
Filling hearts with cosmic ease.

The pulse of suns, a gentle tune,
Awakens dreams beneath the moon.
In every flicker, hope ignites,
As we embrace the starry nights.

Softly we breathe the solar light,
Finding peace in boundless flight.
Each distant sun a guiding spark,
Illuminating paths through dark.

Celestial Hearts in an Endless Dance

Hearts of starlight beating near,
In a cosmic dance, we cheer.
Celestial rhythms draw us close,
In this waltz, we feel the most.

Stars sway gently, a heavenly tune,
In the embrace of night and moon.
Each heartbeat echoes through the night,
Uniting souls in brilliant light.

Galactic spirals spin around,
In harmony, we all are bound.
With every step, the universe glows,
In the dance, true love bestows.

Through the vastness, we entwine,
With cosmic grace, our fates align.
Whispers of love in the endless sky,
Together, forever, you and I.

Oh, how we twirl in timeless grace,
In the grandest, vastest space.
Celestial hearts, we shall embrace,
In this endless, wondrous place.

Secrets Carried on Galactic Winds

Whispers float in the dark, vast space,
Tales of love and time's gentle grace.
Stars twinkle with secrets profound,
Carried softly, without a sound.

Nebulas cradle forgotten dreams,
In cosmic currents, the soul redeems.
Galactic winds, a timeless flow,
Hiding wonders we long to know.

Echoes of laughter from worlds afar,
Each breath of wind, a guiding star.
Constellations weave stories bright,
In the tapestry of endless night.

Planets spin with ancient lore,
In the darkness, the spirits soar.
Hidden truths drift through the skies,
In the dance of time, wisdom lies.

The universe sings a soft refrain,
In every sigh, a sweet, sweet pain.
Secrets linger, waiting to be found,
On galactic winds, they're tightly bound.

The Essence of Night's Embrace

Under a cloak of softest stars,
Night wraps the world in its quiet arms.
Moonlight bathes the trees in silver,
Whispers of dreams that gently quiver.

Shadows dance with the cool night breeze,
Nature's heart beats with tranquil ease.
The sky, a canvas of deep, dark hues,
Painting the night with delicate blues.

Crickets serenade the sleeping earth,
A melody sweet, a song of birth.
In the hush, the cosmos sways,
In night's embrace, the spirit plays.

Stars filter through the velvet veil,
In their glow, old stories unveil.
The essence of night whispers low,
Secrets of life in the moon's soft glow.

In the stillness, the heart finds peace,
As nature's wonders never cease.
Wrapped in night's tender grace,
The world finds solace in its embrace.

Echoing Heartbeats of Distant Stars

In the quiet of the cosmic sea,
Heartbeat echoes, wild and free.
Each pulse a tale of light and fire,
Bringing dreams that never tire.

Galaxies swirl in a dance divine,
Their rhythms thread through space and time.
With every twinkle, stories ignite,
Of journeys taken in deep, dark night.

Every heartbeat sings a song,
Of loss, of love, where we belong.
The universe holds us close and tight,
In mirrored moments of purest light.

Stars whisper truths in timeless tongues,
Where ancient memories still belong.
Each flicker a promise, a sacred trust,
In stardust trails, we find our gust.

As comets blaze across the sky,
In their wake, we question why.
Echoing heartbeats, night alive,
In the vastness, we all strive.

The Dance of Cosmic Memory

In the folds of space, a rhythm flows,
The dance of time where the cosmos knows.
Each star a step in the graceful sway,
Guiding the night, lighting the way.

Planets spin like dancers elegant,
A ballet of fate, seemingly transcendent.
Galactic steps, in patterns wide,
Composing a waltz for all to bide.

Memories linger in the stardust trails,
Silent whispers of forgotten tales.
As dark matter weaves through the vast unknown,
The dance of life continues, grown.

In the twilight glow, the universe breathes,
Uniting all hearts with gentle wreaths.
A cosmic ballet that never fades,
With each twirl, a new path cascades.

The fabric of space spins ever tight,
In the dance of stars, day turns to night.
And in this endless cosmic trance,
We find our place within the dance.

Flickering Dreams of the Cosmos

In the night where shadows play,
Stars whisper secrets from far away.
Thoughts drift softly like cosmic breeze,
Embracing the wonder with gentle ease.

Galaxies swirl in a waltzing dance,
Each spark ignites a fleeting glance.
Across the void, our hopes take flight,
In the silence, we find our light.

Nebulae shimmer in colors so bright,
Painting the canvas of infinite night.
With every twinkle, dreams intertwine,
Woven in starlust, a fate so divine.

Journeying through the astral tide,
We seek the truth that the stars provide.
Merging our souls with the cosmic stream,
Lost in the flicker of everlasting dream.

Here in the vastness, our spirits roam,
Eternal wanderers, forever home.
In the tapestry of the universe's seam,
We find our purpose in flickering dreams.

Songs of Starlight Whispers

In the hush of night, a song takes flight,
Whispers of starlight weave pure delight.
Melodies dance on the soft lunar glow,
Guiding our hearts where the shadows grow.

Each note a beacon, each chord a spark,
Illuminating the silence, igniting the dark.
Through the void, echoes of love we share,
Resonating softly in the cool night air.

Constellations hum in a cosmic choir,
Filling the heavens with celestial fire.
Dreamers unite under shimmering skies,
Finding their voice where the starlight lies.

With every breath, the universe sings,
A harmony woven with ancient strings.
We chase the rhythms across time and space,
In songs of starlight, we find our place.

Together we sway to the cosmic tune,
Beneath the watchful gaze of the moon.
In the serenade of the night's sweet kiss,
We lose ourselves in starlight bliss.

Illuminated Paths of Remembrance

In twilight's embrace, we wander slow,
Tracing the footprints of long ago.
Each step a memory wrapped in light,
Guiding us gently through the depth of night.

Flickering lanterns dot the unseen way,
Echoing laughter of those who stay.
Through corridors of time, we glide,
On illuminated paths where dreams abide.

Faces from the past beam like the sun,
Reminders of battles lost and won.
Carving their stories in the heart's soft clay,
Illuminated whispers that never stray.

With every shadow stretching long,
The ties of love create our song.
Together we walk with souls so dear,
In paths of remembrance, we feel them near.

The glow of our journey lights the night,
Binding the lost with our lives so bright.
In the dance of memories, we find our peace,
As illuminated paths lead us to release.

A Journey through Celestial Echoes

Time stretches out in a cosmic embrace,
Each moment a star in the vastness of space.
We ride the waves of celestial sound,
In echoes of silence, our truth is found.

Across the expanse where dreams collide,
We sail on stardust, a cosmic tide.
With hearts wide open, we wander afar,
Tracing the trails of each glowing star.

Galactic whispers weave tales of old,
In cosmic libraries where mysteries unfold.
The past intertwines with the future's flight,
In the journey through echoes, we find our light.

Every heartbeat syncs with the universe's pulse,
Resonating through galaxies, vast and dulcet.
In the dance of the cosmos, we seek and roam,
Finding in echoes a place we call home.

As the echoes fade into the quiet night,
We carry their warmth as we take our flight.
In the tapestry of time, forever we roam,
On a journey through echoes, together, we're home.